ETHICS IN SERVICE

ETHICS IN SERVICE

BY

WILLIAM HOWARD TAFT

KENNIKAT PRESS
Port Washington, N. Y./London

ETHICS IN SERVICE

PREFACE

The legal profession discharges a most important function in a civilized community, and it seems to me that a discussion of the ethics and ideals of that profession would come within the purpose of the Page foundation, which is described by the donor as intended to promote "the ethical side of business life, including the morals and ethics of public service." I shall first ask your attention to the history of the profession, which shows that a paid advocacy is the only practical system, and to the rules of conduct to which lawyers must be held in order that such a system shall promote justice. I cannot claim to have any peculiar knowledge upon this subject other than that derived from a somewhat brief practice of five years at the Bar, from an experience of eleven years on the Bench of trial and appellate courts, from a somewhat varied experience in the responsibility of government, not only in this country, but in those far-distant isles of the Pacific in which the United States has been grafting the principles of free government upon a civilization inherited from Spain.

CONTENTS

ETHICS IN SERVICE

CHAPTER I

HISTORY OF THE PROFESSION OF LAW

I⊤ is not too much to say that the profession of the law is more or less on trial. It is certain that there is a crisis in the life of our courts, and that a great political issue is being forced upon the people, for they must decide whether the courts are to continue to exercise the power they now have, and what character of service they shall be required to render. Judges are lawyers. They ought to be trained practitioners and learned in the profession of the law before they ascend the Bench, and generally they are. Therefore, our courts, as they are now conducted, and our profession, which is the handmaid of justice, are necessarily so bound together in our judicial system that an attack upon the courts is an attack upon our profession, and an attack upon our profession is equally an attack upon the courts.

We have all noted on the stage and in the current literature the flippant and sarcastic references to the failures of the administration of justice, and we are familiar with the sometimes insidious and too often open impeachments of the

courts, which appear in the press and upon the
hustings. They are charged with failure to do
justice, with bad faith, with lack of intelligent
sympathy for socially progressive movements,
with a rigid and reactionary obstruction to the
movement toward greater equality of condition,
and with a hidebound and unnecessarily sensitive
attitude of mind in respect to the rights of property. One count that looms large in the wide
range of the indictment against our judicial
system is the immoral part that lawyers are said
necessarily to play in the perversion of justice
by making the worse appear the better reason.
Such a public agitation and such an issue in
politics lead to a consideration of the fundamental
reasons for the existence of our profession in the
past, and a further inquiry as to the need for it
in the future, as preliminary to a discussion of
the rules of conduct that should govern its
practice.

There are those who intimate that we can learn
nothing from the past. They don't say so in so
many words, but they proceed on the theory that
man, under the elevating influences with which
they propose to surround him, is suddenly to
become a different creature, prompted by different
motives. But those of us who have been fortunate
in having an education permeated with an atmosphere of common sense, and an idea of how to

deal with human nature as it is, realize that the world is not to be reformed tomorrow or in a month or a year or in a century, but that progress is to be made slowly and that the problems before us are not so widely different from those which were presented to our ancestors as far back as the Christian era. Nor can we fail to derive some benefit from a consideration of such troubles, tribulations and triumphs of our profession in the past as suggest rules of conduct for lawyers in the future. I do not mean that we are not to aspire for better things. Nor do I wish to deny us the happiness of hope for reasonable and real progress toward higher ideals. I simply insist that we ought not to ignore the lessons of experience when we deal with conditions as they are and as everybody who is familiar with them knows them to be.

The three civilizations in which we may most profitably study the growth and development of the legal profession are the Jewish, the Roman and the English. Among the Jews, the Mosaic law, which went into the smallest details of personal life, was the guide to their rule of action. As it had religious sanction, the high priests became the actual ministers of justice and the preservation of religion and law was united in them. Acting as their assistants, and as assessors in the tribunals of which the high priests were the head, were the Scribes. They were learned in the law; had a religious and priestly character themselves; interpreted the Mosaic law with a view to its application to the various facts and issues which arose; and were in addition the teachers of law. It was to them that the rabbinical injunction was made "to make the knowledge of the law neither a crown wherewith to make a show, nor a spade wherewith to dig." And again it was said, "He who uses the crown of the law for external aims fades away."

In describing the principles of non-remuneration to the Scribes, the learned German Professor Schurer says: "In Christ's censures of the Scribes and Pharisees, their covetousness is a special object of reproof. Hence, even if their instruction was given gratuitously, they certainly knew how to compensate themselves in some other way." And it is because of this evasion of this rule that we find those passages in the eleventh chapter of Luke, the 46th and 52d verses, which read:

Verse 46. "And he said, Woe unto you also, ye lawyers! for ye lade men with burdens grievous to be borne, and ye yourselves touch not the burdens with one of your fingers."

Verse 52. "Woe unto you, lawyers! for ye have taken away the key of knowledge: ye entered not in yourselves, and them that were entering in ye hindered.''

The line between the judicial and advisory functions of the Hebrew Scribes was not closely or clearly drawn. They were evidently supposed to occupy a disinterested position toward those who consulted them and to be in a sense the associates of the judges. Since the motive which prompted their study of particular cases was supposed to be only that of vindicators of general justice, the rules which nominally guided their action, as announced by the lawgivers, required that their services should always be gratuitous. But quite naturally their consultation with private litigants prompted such litigants to influence their view of the law, and command their skill in debate. And so to evade the rule which prevented remuneration they established the custom of giving presents in advance. These presents given in advance to secure the kindly favor of the Scribes are interesting as the precursors of that institution dear to every English barrister, and not unknown—nor even objectionable—to American lawyers, to wit, the Retainer. In fact it was the impossibility of finding men who could remain judicial in their attitude when the thought of remuneration moved them to advocate the cause of one of the litigants, that put the Scribes of those days in an indefensible position and led to the attacks upon them that we find in the New Testament.

And so it was in Rome. There the progenitor of the lawyer was first the priest, the *Pontifex,* mingling judicial and advisory functions, and then the *patronus* or the orator, a man of wealth and high standing in the community, who had gathered about him freed men and Plebeians as his supporters. The latter were known as his *clientes,* from which term our word is derived. When one of his clients became involved in a lawsuit, the *patronus* appeared to advise the judge— a magistrate acting only as vindicator of general justice and often not learned in the principles of law—and was not supposed to receive any compensation. Less than the *patronus,* but exercising similar functions, was the *advocatus*—who, though perhaps not so learned in the law, nor so formidable as a person, was able to assist the *patronus* before the tribunal on behalf of others. There was in addition a body of men called "jurist consults," learned in the law and able to advise, who came to be recognized as the members of a select profession in the time of Augustus.

In the year 200 before Christ, the Cincian law was enacted, requiring that service of the *patronus* and the advocate should be gratuitous, but it was soon evaded even as the Jewish laws had been.

Again presents were made to secure the skilled advocacy of men learned in the law and acute in debate. These gifts like the Hebrew ones were paid in advance and were called "honorariums," another term which suggests the modern retainer. Neither an *advocatus* nor a *patronus* could sue for such honorarium at law because it was a violation of law, but once paid, the honorarium could not be recovered. Cicero boasted that he never violated the Cincian law, but historians of his period intimate that by secret loans and testamentary gifts his practice proved to be very profitable. And it is certain, at least, that many of his contemporaries were made very rich by professional remuneration. Augustus directed the passage of another law forbidding compensation to orators and advocates, but it was disregarded and subsequent emperors contented themselves with fixing limits for the fees to be charged. In the golden age of the Roman law, therefore, the payment of the profession became recognized as legitimate and the profession itself became a definite body with clearly understood functions.

In England, for two hundred years after the Conquest, the priests were the only learned men, and they, too, like the Scribes, acted as judges and advisers of litigants. Even as late as the time of Henry VIII, as we know, the Keeper of the King's Conscience and the head of the Court of

Equity, was an Ecclesiastic in the formidable person of Cardinal Woolsey. About the reign of King John, laymen became lawyers, and in Henry III's time the Pope forbade priests to fit themselves in civil law or to act as advisers in respect to it. We may properly say that the profession of the Bar, as a recognized English institution, had its beginnings in the struggle for individual rights by which the English race forced the great charter from King John. We find that in the history of the early English administration of justice, bailiffs, undersheriffs, clerical attachés and the underlings of the courts had gone into the business of acting as attorneys, of cheating their clients, and of stirring up litigation. While statutes were directed against their abuses, I cannot find that there was any English statute forbidding lawyers to receive compensation for their services, although the action of the Pope in forbidding his priests to study and practice law in England may indicate some such abuses. It is certain that legal services were not regarded as creating a debt due from the client to the lawyer who had served him. By statute, now, attorneys and solicitors in England are entitled to fixed fees for professional services. But in the case of barristers, down to the present time, while they may demand a retainer for their services in advance, they still cannot recover by suit if the services are rendered without receiving it. This may possibly be derived from the early Roman and Jewish view of the professional relation and suggests the probability that early in English history professional services were deemed to be gratuitous.

The grant of Magna Charta by King John, in response to the demand of the Barons at Runnymede, gave birth to the Bar in its modern character. Articles 17 and 18 of that instrument provided that Common Pleas should not follow the court of the King, but should be held in a certain place, and that trials upon certain writs should not be taken outside of their proper counties. It provided further that the King or the Chief Justice should send two justiciaries into each county, four times in the year, to hold certain assizes within the county, with four knights of the county, chosen by it, on the day, and at the place appointed. The 45th article promised that the King would not make Justiciaries, Constables, or Bailiffs excepting of such as knew the laws of the land and were well disposed to observe them. The result of this provision by which Common pleas courts came to be held at Westminster, while regular assizes were held in the counties, was the establishment of the four Inns of Court, so-called, Lincoln's Inn, the Inner and the Middle Temple, and Gray's Inn,

together with a number of others known as
Chancery Inns, which have of late years dis-
appeared. Henry III took these Inns under his
especial protection and prohibited the study of
law anywhere in London save in the Inns of Court.
They were the homes of the Bar, for within their
walls lawyers had their offices, and there students
of the law received their education. In fact, they
may be said to constitute the foundation of the
modern profession of the law in the English-
speaking race.

The Inns of Court were at first an aristocratic
institution, and only men of good blood were permitted to practice in them. Indeed, that was the
case in the early days in Rome. Pliny reports
that no one could become a *jurist consult*, an
advocatus or a *patronus* except he be of the Patri-
cian class. But soon after the Empire began,
this rule broke down and the Roman Bar became
open to all. So, too, in the English Bar at first
admission was controlled by the Benchers or
governing bodies of the Inns of Court and the
students were chosen only from good families.
It was probably this that led to their unpopularity
and to the denunciation which they received in
Wat Tyler's day, in the fourteenth century, and
from Jack Cade's followers whom Shakespeare
makes wish to kill all the lawyers in the next
century. Their exclusive spirit passed away,

however, and while aristocratic class distinctions were rigidly maintained in English society, the Bar became most democratic through the avenue to positions of highest influence on the Bench and in politics which it freely offered to able men from the people. And, indeed, there is no part of English history that is so full of interest as the stories of her great lawyers, who, beginning in the humblest conditions of life, fought their way by real merit into positions of control in the government and thus gave ability and strength to the aristocracy of which they became a part.

In the three centuries or more after the establishment of the Inns of Court, no division appeared in the profession of the law, and it was not until about 1556 that the profession became separated into attorneys at law and solicitors in chancery, on the one hand, and barristers on the other. The former dealt directly with clients and performed the preliminary work of drafting documents and preparing briefs, while the latter, the barristers, drafted the pleadings and presented the causes in court. A similar division of functions prevailed in the Roman Bar. I shall have occasion later to comment on the advantages and disadvantages of this division, but this summary reference is sufficient for my present purpose in tracing the history of the Bar in England.

During this period, after the establishment of the Inns of Court, the unpopularity of the Bar manifested itself in the enactment of statutes forbidding the election of lawyers to Parliament. This gave rise to the noted Parliament known as the "Dunces Parliament," because everybody who knew anything about the law, and therefore about the framing or the operation of statutes, was excluded from membership.

In his interesting history of the American Bar, Mr. Charles Warren, of the Boston Bar, says:

"Lawyers, as the instruments through which the subtleties and iniquities of the Common Law were enforced, were highly unpopular as a class in England during the period of Cromwell and Milton."

Milton wrote:

"Most men are allured to the trade of law, grounding their purposes not on the prudent and heavenly contemplation of justice and equity, which was never taught them, but on the promising and pleasing thoughts of litigious terms, fat contentions and flowing fees."

As examples of a lawyer's reputation in London in the seventeenth century, Mr. Warren cites the titles of the following tracts printed at that time: "The Downfall of Unjust Lawyers"; "Doomsday

Drawing Near with Thunder and Lightning for Lawyers"; "A Rod for Lawyers who are Hereby declared Robbers and Deceivers of the Nation"; "Essay where is Described the Lawyers, Smugglers and Officers Frauds."

I note these facts as I progress to indicate and reinforce my original statement that the present time is not the only time in the history of civilization when lawyers have received the condemnation of their fellow subjects or fellow citizens. Yet not only has the profession survived such movements but its usefulness has been recognized in succeeding crises.

I need hardly mention that most of the progress toward individual liberty in English history was made through the successful struggle of the lawyers against the assertion of the divine right of Kings and through the defence of privilege by members of our profession. Lawyers like Lord Coke and Lord Hale stand out in the profession for their maintenance of the independence of the judiciary and their support of the liberties of subjects. The great charters, the Petition of Right, the Habeas Corpus Act, the Bill of Rights, and the Acts of Settlement, establishing the judiciary independent of Royal control, were obtained at the instance of lawyers who knew better than any other class the absolute necessity for such reforms in the maintenance of free institutions.

The evolution of the Bar in this country during colonial times—especially in New England—was a curious counterpart of the history of the English Bar three centuries before. The founders of New England came here to escape a persecution for their religious beliefs and law was closely connected in their minds with the injustices, the inequalities and the rigid hardships of the common law as administered by judges appointed and removable at the will of the Tudors and Stuarts. At that time lawyers exercising their profession were the instruments of a system that had become non-progressive. They had lost the principles of justice in technicalities and had become mere political tools in the hands of tyrants. But in England, the law soon lost its narrowing, hard and inflexible character through the intervention of courts of equity and through the genius and broad views of great judges of common law like Mansfield. It was modified further by the civil law and by the needs of a developing world commerce, and after the action of the Long Parliament and the Revolution it was no longer used as an instrument of tyranny.

In this country, however, the Puritans and the Pilgrims approved of neither the common law nor the English judicial system, and as lawyers were only part of that system, they considered the abolition of the profession from their society as an end devoutly to be wished for and promptly sought. Among the Pilgrim fathers there was not a single lawyer, while among the Puritans there were only four or five who had been educated as lawyers and even they had never practiced. The consequence was that during the seventeenth century and far into the eighteenth, lawyers had little place in the social or political institutions of the colonies. In New England there was a theocracy. The judges—none of them lawyers—were all either ministers or directly under the influence of the clergy. A colonial common law grew up among them, based on a theological reasoning and was really administered without lawyers. In the Massachusetts body of liberties, it was provided that a man unfit to plead might employ a person not objectionable to the Court to plead for him, on condition that he give him no fee or reward. In 1663 a usual or common attorney was prohibited from sitting in the general court.

As society progressed, however, as commerce and trade increased, as wealth grew, as business transactions became more extended and as learning spread from the clergy to other persons, opportunity and inducement were furnished for the study of the law, and professional training

became more general. The crying need for a
learned and honorable profession of the law was
made manifest by the growth of a class of advocates and advisers whose influence was most
pernicious. Litigants needed guidance in the presentation of their cases and no learned profession
being available, the underbailiffs, undersheriffs,
clerks and other underlings of the administration
of justice began to practice, without real knowledge. Greedy and lacking in principle, they
developed trickery and stirred up litigation for
their own profit, just as their predecessors had
done three hundred years before in England.
Colonial statutes were then passed, forbidding
such underlings of the court to practice law at all.
But lawyers were not popular in colonial days
even after the Bar became able and respectable.
In fact a bitter spirit was manifested against
lawyers even as late as Shays's Rebellion after
the Revolutionary War.

Between the years 1750 and 1775, more than a
hundred and fifty young men from the colonies
were admitted to one of the four Inns of Court
and became educated lawyers with the purpose
of entering the profession in their native colonies.
How far the presence of such a class of educated
lawyers through the colonies contributed to the
resentment against the stupidity and injustice of
the English colonial policy which brought about

the Revolution, cannot be estimated exactly; but certain it is that the preparation of the lawyers who were then in their prime appears to have been Providential interference in behalf of the people of the United States. Never in history has the profession of the law received so great a harvest of profound students of the constitutional principles of government as did our country at this time. Our lawyers signed the Declaration of Independence, served in the Continental Congress, acted as delegates to the Constitutional Convention, and met in the various conventions called by the states to consider the ratification of that great instrument. They not only knew that common law, but they had studied closely the political history of Greece and Rome, and were familiar with the principles of government as set forth by Montesquieu and Adam Smith.

It was the American Bar that gave to the people of the United States such lawyers as Alexander Hamilton, John Jay, James Madison, George Mason, Thomas Jefferson, Patrick Henry, John Adams, James Otis, Samuel Chase, Samuel Adams, Roger Sherman, Oliver Ellsworth, James Wilson, Edmund Randolph and many others not less learned and brilliant, to establish their liberties, frame the limitations of their government and care for the protection of individual rights. The same Bar furnished a little later that lawyer and judge, John Marshall, whose interpretation of the Constitution was as important in its beneficent effect as its original framing. That Bar not only helped largely in constructing the ship of state but it was also most instrumental in launching it on a triumphant and useful course through a century and a quarter. The profound gratitude of succeeding generations owing to such a Bar ought never to be dimmed by partisan or misguided diatribes upon lawyers and judges.

CHAPTER II

LEGAL ETHICS

I HAVE heard the utility of legal ethics denied. It is said that the rules in legal ethics are the same as the moral rules that govern men in every branch of society and in every profession—except as there may be certain conventions as to professional etiquette—and that if a man is honest, there ought to be no difficulty in his following the right course in the discharge of his professional duties. If a man is lacking in probity of character, it is said the discussion of legal ethics will do him no particular good, because if he is tempted to a crooked path or an unjust act by his pecuniary interest, he will yield, and neither lectures on ethics nor the establishment of an ethical code will make him good; whereas the upright man will either not be so tempted, or should he be, he will clearly perceive the necessity for resisting the temptation.

In the course of my consideration of this subject, I looked into a text-book on moral philosophy and the general system of ethics with the hope that I might find something there that would suggest, by analogy, a proper treatment of the subject in hand. I consulted Paulsen's "A System of Ethics." The analogy between moral philosophy and legal ethics is not very close, but I found a passage or two bearing on this very issue, which it seems to me might not be inappropriately quoted here. In the conclusion of his introduction, Paulsen says:

"Let me say a word concerning the *practical value* of ethics. Can ethics be a practical science, not only in the sense that it deals with practice, but that it influences practice? This was its original purpose. 'It is the function of ethics,' says Aristotle, 'to act, not only to theorize.'"

Paulsen refers to the fact that Schopenhauer takes a different view:

"All philosophy," he says, "is theoretical. Upon mature reflection it ought finally to abandon the old demand that it become practical, guide action, and transform character, for here it is not dead concepts that decide, but the innermost essence of the human being, the demon that guides him. It is as impossible to teach virtue as it is to teach genius. It would be as foolish to expect our moral systems to produce virtuous characters and saints as to expect the science of æsthetics to bring forth poets, sculptors and musicians."

To this view Paulsen replies:

"I do not believe that ethics need be so faint-hearted. Its first object, it is true, is to understand human strivings and modes of conduct, conditions and institutions, as well as their effects upon individual and social life. But if knowledge is capable of influencing conduct—which Schopenhauer himself would not deny—it is hard to understand why the knowledge of ethics alone should be fruitless in this respect. . . . Moral instruction, however, can have no practical effect unless there be some agreement concerning the nature of the final goal—not a mere verbal agreement, to be sure, but one based upon actual feeling. . . . It will be the business of ethics to invite the doubter and the inquirer to assist in the common effort to discover fixed principles which shall help the judgment to understand the aims and problems of life."

What is here said concerning the usefulness of an investigation of fixed ethical principles has application to a consideration of what rules of conduct should prevail in the legal profession. The high social purpose of the profession, its beneficial function, and the limitations upon its action that should be self-enforced in order to make the calling an advantage and not a detriment to the public weal, should be understood. Indeed, the profession of the law, if it serves its high purpose, and vindicates its existence, requires a double allegiance from those who have assumed its obligations, first, a duty toward their clients, and second, a duty toward the court. And though the two sometimes seem to conflict, they must be reconciled in the way which will best promote the effective administration of justice and the peace of society. The path to be followed in achieving this golden mean in the intricacies of professional relations is not as manifest as the rule of honesty and morality in ordinary life. The great problem of government that is never completely solved and that is changing with changing conditions is how to reconcile the protection of individual rights, helpful to the pursuit of happiness and the welfare of society, with the necessary curtailment of those rights and freedom, by governmental restriction, to achieve the same object. So the adjustment of the duties of the lawyer toward his client and toward the court in the interest of society, are not always easily distinguishable and an attempt to make them clear, therefore, is justified.

An understanding between the client and his representative that remuneration is a proper incident to their relation insures a greater confidence in the activity and devotion of his lawyer to his interest on the part of the client and

stimulates industry and sincere effort on the part
of the lawyer. It is far better that the employment on a pecuniary basis should be understood
by all men, by the courts and by the parties, than
that some secret arrangements should exist unknown to the court and the opposing party. But
it is said that to give to counsel, skilled, learned
and familiar with the arts of advocacy and the
preparation of cases, a pecuniary motive to make
the worse appear the better reason, necessarily
leads him to an attempt to influence the court
against a just result. For since one or the other
conclusion must be unjust, one of the paid attorneys arguing the cause before the court must be
arguing for the unjust side and in favor of wrong.
Hence, it is claimed, the system of paid advocacy
must in every case tend to an effort on one side
or the other to pervert justice and mislead the
judges into inequity and wrong.

It may be agreed that if there were not certain
limitations upon the means which counsel may
take to maintain the justice of their clients' cause,
if they were justified in suborning witnesses, and
coaching them to testify to an unfounded state of
facts, if they were permitted to misstate the
evidence after it has been adduced, if it were
regarded as proper for them to accept employment in the prosecution of a cause which they
knew to be brought only for a wrong purpose and

without any just foundation, or if in a civil cause
they were retained to make a defence which they
were advised was false and wrong, then it might
be that advocacy under such freedom from limitation would not aid the judges in avoiding wrong
conclusions and unjust judgments. But there are
limitations upon the duty of counsel to their
clients. There are also limitations upon a lawyer's action which he cannot violate without a
breach of his duty to the court of which he is an
officer and to the public interest in the maintenance of the proper administration of justice.
We find, therefore, that the goal to be reached in
reference to the ethical duty of an attorney in the
discharge of the functions assigned to him by
the law, is the reconciliation of his duty to his
client, with his duty to the court. To mark out
this line in advance is easier than to determine
each special duty in a concrete way, yet neither
is free from difficulty and each requires a calm
and clear understanding of the function of counsel
as an instrument in the machinery of justice.
This is the main object of legal ethics. It covers
other fields and is important in those fields, but no
other is of such primary importance.

Courts sit to hear controversies between parties
over facts and law. Rules of procedure are for
the purpose of reducing the issues of fact and law
in such controversies to a form as narrow and

concrete as possible. Men who are able to present a clear statement of the evidence and who are learned in the principles of the law and their application to the facts as they are developed are in a position to assist the judge to a quick and thorough understanding of the exact question which he is to decide. The real enthusiasm of advocacy which is necessarily developed by the relation of attorney and client would doubtless have a tendency to mislead the court if exerted in behalf of one side only, but where both sides are represented, where the same earnestness in the proceeding of each side is present, it is the best method within human ken to reach a sound conclusion both as to the facts and as to the law. No one who has had experience on the Bench in reaching judicial conclusions and who has thereafter been obliged in an executive position to reach important, and it may be final, conclusions upon questions involving both fact and law, can fail to recognize and acknowledge the powerful influence for justice that honorable and learned members of the law exert in the causes which they present to a court. The counsel who argues the losing side of a case contributes quite as much to the assistance of the court as the successful advocate. The friction of counsel's argument against counsel's argument develops every phase of possible error in a conclusion and thereby enables a just, intelligent, acute and experienced court to see clearly what is the right which should be embodied in its judgment.

The practical value of argument by paid counsel on both sides is shown in many ways. In the first place, it is well understood in weighing legal precedents that there is little authority in the decision of a court which has been reached without the benefit of the argument of counsel. In some states, courts are required to answer questions from the legislature as to the constitutionality of proposed laws. The best authorities hold that opinions given under such circumstances are merely advisory, since they lack opposing arguments made by counsel whom the spirit of professional advocacy arouses to industry in the search for precedent. They go so far as to say that answers so given should not conclude the same court in a litigated case arising subsequently. An earnest and commendable desire to win leads the counsel to search not only libraries but his own brain for the strongest reasons that he can summon upon which to base a judgment in behalf of his client. Why is it that a great Bar makes a great court? Though it may seem a truism, I repeat, it is because the great Bar furnishes to the court all the reasons that can possibly be urged in each case and enables it to select from among all the reasons developed by the ingenuity and intense interest of men skilled in the law.

Counsel ought to decline to conduct a civil cause or to make a defence when convinced that it is intended merely to harass the opposite party or to work oppression. His appearance in court should, therefore, be deemed equivalent to an assertion on his honor that in his opinion his client's case is a debatable one and one proper for judicial determination. He should know that under a proper code of ethics, no lawyer is obliged to act either as adviser or as advocate for every person who may wish to become his client; that he has the right to decline employment, and that each lawyer on his own responsibility must decide what business he will accept as counsel, what causes he will bring into court for plaintiffs, and what suits he will contest in court for defence. The court knows that the responsibility for bringing questionable suits or for urging questionable defences, is the lawyer's responsibility. He can not escape it by urging as an excuse that he is only following his client's instruction. The judge knows that no honorable lawyer would coach a witness to testify falsely, and that in dealing with the court each lawyer is required to act with entire candor and fairness in the statements upon which he invokes its action. The judge knows that it would not be candid or fair for the lawyer knowingly to misquote the contents of a paper, the testimony of a witness, the argument of opposing counsel, the language of a decision, or the wording of a text-book. He may fairly rely on a lawyer not to cite a decision that he knows has been overruled, or a statute that he knows has been repealed. He may properly rely on the counsel's not asserting a fact that has not been proven.

Yet he knows that lawyers owe entire devotion to the interest of the client, and warm zeal in the maintenance of his rights and that they will exert their utmost ability lest anything be taken or be withheld from him, save by the rules of law, legally applied. He knows that counsel has the right to proceed in the view that his client is entitled to the benefit of every remedy and defence authorized by the law of the land and that the lawyer is expected to assert every such remedy or defence. But it is steadfastly to be borne in mind that the great trust to the lawyer is to be formed within and not without the bounds of the law. The office of a lawyer does not permit, much less does it demand of him, violation of law or any manner of fraud for any client. He must obey his own conscience and not that of his client. These limitations are binding upon the lawyer as a sworn officer of the court, and compliance with them is the true reconciliation of the primary duty of fidelity to the client, with the constant and ever present duty owing to the minister of justice in the person of the judge. These statements of the duty of the lawyer to the court in the advocacy of causes and in the presentation of his client's case, are taken from the Code of Legal Ethics, which was approved by the American Bar Association. I think that all lawyers and judges will agree that when lawyers live up to them, the danger of injustice from the enthusiasm, skill or eloquence of their advocacy is quite remote.

I don't mean to say that lawyers do not differ in the force of their statements, in their logical faculty, in their method of arranging arguments, in their fluency and in the cogency with which they present the cause of their respective clients. Of course the man who is fortunate enough to engage the abler lawyer enjoys the advantage of those gifts with which nature has endowed his representative, but that element of inequality can hardly be eliminated from the administration of justice. It has more weight in a jury trial than it has before a court, for the lawyers before a court are matching their acuteness and learning not alone with the counsel for the other side, but with the cold scrutiny of a calm, intellectual and judicial mind, trained to consider argument, and experienced in the elimination of the irrelevant, the emotional and the illogical.

The jury system, though somewhat crude and not always certain, has advantages that outweigh its possibility of injustice in the judicial system of a free government among a free people. It is important that the people shall have confidence in the courts, and it is important that they shall feel that they may themselves be a part of the judicial machinery. The value of popular confidence in the verdict of a jury selected at random from a community is great enough to offset any tendency to error that may at times arise from the undue influence of a jury advocate upholding one side of the controversy before them. If the jury is misled by the histrionic eloquence of counsel so that it clearly violates justice in its verdict, the court may always set aside its decision and give a new trial. Moreover, in any properly adjusted system, the judge should be able to clear the atmosphere of any false emotion that counsel may have created. He can remind the jury in his charge that they are judges, who may not indulge their emotions or their prejudices. He should follow closely the argument of counsel to the jury in order that his charge may clear up the evidence by inviting the attention of the jury to the weakness of proof at critical points of the cause, or by pointing out either the bias

of witnesses or their opportunity or lack of it for
observation, thereby eliminating those phases of
the controversy that the earnestness of counsel
may have seized upon to divert the attention of
the jury from the real issue.

I have recently heard an arraignment of our
present judicial system in the trial of causes by
a prominent, able and experienced member of the
Boston Bar. (I am glad to call him a friend. I
value him highly as such.) He ascribes what he
calls the growing lack of confidence in the justice
and equity of litigation in the courts to the fundamental error in their procedure. He feels that
the procedure now in vogue authorizes and in
fact requires counsel to withhold facts from the
court which would help the cause of justice if
they were brought out by his own statement. To
remedy this he suggests that all counsel should
be compelled to disclose any facts communicated
to them by their clients which would require a
decision of the case against the clients. He
contends further that the rules of procedure,
which exclude hearsay evidence, and prevent the
jury from hearing many facts which business men
regard as important evidence, make it difficult
to reach the truth which is essential to justice.

I set out this view as a possible basis for a
discussion of the grounds for popular criticism
of the courts. To require the counsel to disclose

the confidential communications of his client to the very court and jury which are to pass on the issue which he is making, would end forever the possibility of any useful relation between lawyer and client. It is essential for the proper presentation of the client's cause that he should be able to talk freely with his counsel without fear of disclosure. This has always been recognized and has acted as a most salutary restriction on the conduct of counsel. No litigants, or intending litigants, would employ counsel if the latter were to assume the duty of extracting from their clients all their innermost thoughts with a view to revealing them to the court. The useful function of lawyers is not only to conduct litigation but to avoid it, where possible, by advising settlement or withholding suit. Thus, any rule that interfered with the complete disclosure of the client's inmost thoughts on the issue he presents would seriously obstruct the peace that is gained for society by the compromises which the counsel is able to advise.

The objection to the exclusion of hearsay evidence is equally unfounded. Its uses are said to be threefold, to convince in affairs of the world, to serve as the basis of action for business men, and to prevent opportunity for false witness. Yet it is not admissible in a court of justice to prove or disprove either a cause or a defence.

The rules of evidence have been worked out by centuries of experience of courts in jury trials, and are admirably adapted to avoid the danger of error as to fact. I fully agree that in American courts the trial judges have not been entrusted with as wide discretion in the matter of admitting or rejecting evidence as they should have, and judgments have been reversed on technical errors in admitting testimony which should have been affirmed. As time goes on, however, the rule against hearsay evidence, instead of losing its force, is demonstrating its usefulness. The error and injustice that are committed in the public press by inaccurate, garbled and sometimes false statements of facts are increased in their injurious effect by the wider publication that newspapers have today, and the requirement that when a fact is to be proven in court it should be proven by those who have a personal knowledge of it, is one of the most wholesome and searching tests of truth that the whole range of adjective law furnishes. The opportunity for cross-examination, for finding out the bias of the witness, the advantage or disadvantage of his point of observation, the accuracy or inaccuracy in his recollection of the details of what he saw, are all means of reaching the real truth that the introduction of hearsay evidence would entirely exclude.

It is now more than fifteen years since this

country was following with bated breath the judicial investigation of the charges against Captain Dreyfus for treason in having sold secrets of the French War Office to Germany. Under the civil law procedure, there is little, if any, limitation upon the kind of evidence which can be introduced to sustain the issue on either side, and the rule against hearsay evidence does not prevail. The shock given to the whole community of the United States by the character of evidence received to help the court determine the Dreyfus issue, was itself enough to show that the confidence of the public in the justice of the rule against hearsay evidence had grown rather than diminished with years.

Yet I am far from saying that we may not have improvement in our laws concerning testimony in court. The protection of those accused of crime contained in some of our constitutional restrictions may be too great. The charge against the administration of justice in the present system is that it is nothing but a game of wits, of cunning, and of concealment, promoted by the rules of procedure. I think this characterization is most unjust and most unwise because it aids the attack on a valuable and indispensable institution without suggesting any real security for such evils and defects as there are. An experience of many years in the trial of all sorts of causes as lawyer and judge and in framing a judicial system convinces me that the present method of hearing causes is correct. The enthusiastic advocacy of counsel when they are properly restrained as above suggested, and the rules of evidence adapted to winnowing out the false from the true, are admirably adapted to bringing about right results.

It is also asked whether members of the Bar live up to these rules restraining their enthusiasm and limiting their proper conduct in the advocacy of their clients' causes. One can reply that counsel differ in that regard, but that generally such rules are fairly well observed. The earnestness of advocacy often blinds them to the proprieties and the requirements of candor and fairness. They fall into the same errors that their clients do, though with a better knowledge of their duties in this regard. They share what has been characteristic of our entire people in the last two decades. The minds of the great majority have been focused on business success, on the chase for the dollar, where success seems to have justified some departure from the strict line of propriety or fairness, so long as it has not brought on criminal prosecution or public denunciation.

More than this, the tendency of legislatures, too often controlled by lawyers engaged in active practice, has been to distrust judges and to take away from them the power to control in the court room, as they do in the English and Federal courts. This has had a tendency to transfer to counsel greater discretion in respect to their conduct of cases and greater opportunity to depart from ethical rules with impunity in the somewhat reckless spirit of the times. The hampered power of the court to prevent the misconduct of counsel in many western states has not been conducive to certainty of justice nor has it been of a character to strengthen public confidence in just results. We find the bitterest attacks upon the administration of justice in those jurisdictions in which the people and the legislatures have themselves laid the foundation for the very abuses they subsequently criticise by taking away the power of the judge.

CHAPTER III

THE EXECUTIVE POWER

I HAVE been introduced at a great many places by the exuberant chairman of a committee who referred to the fact that he was about to introduce a gentleman who exercised the greatest power in the world. While the power of the President may be very great as compared with the power of rulers of other countries, I can testify that when you are exercising it, you don't think of its extent so much as you do of its limitations. I think a study of the relative power of the King of England, the President of France, the Emperor of Germany, the King of Italy, the Emperor of Austria and the Emperor of Russia might involve a very interesting investigation. I am not sufficiently familiar with the power of those executive heads to speak on the subject, though I do know something of the power of the King of England. In England and all of her colonies they have a so-called responsible government. The English King is said to reign and not to rule, while the actual ruler is the Premier, who combines executive and legislative power by virtue of his position as head of the controlling party in Parliament. When the legislative majority fails him, he goes out of office. It is a government responsible both for legislation and for executive work.

With us, as you know, the President is a permanent officer for four years. It is quite possible that he may be elected as President at the same time that a Congress hostile to him is put into power. Such was the case when Mr. Hayes was elected, and indeed when Mr. Cleveland was first elected there was a majority against him in the Senate. It happens more frequently, however, that at the end of two years a majority of the opposing party is elected to a Congress at the mid-term election. Our method has been criticised as rigid and unresponsive to change in popular opinion, but I venture to think that it has some advantages over the English one. It may be good for a country to have an occasional rest from legislation, to let it digest what reformers have already gotten on its statute book, and the period when the President differs from Congress offers such an opportunity for test and rest. We have rests in music, which are necessary to a proper composition, and I do not see why we should not have rests in politics.

I think, however, that we might advantageously give greater power to the President in the matter of legislation. One of the difficulties about a Congress—I say it with deference to that body—is that it does not know enough about the executive facts which ought to control legislation in the course of an efficient government. The introduction of cabinet officers on the floor of the House and the floor of the Senate to urge legislation on the one hand, and to point out the defects of proposed legislation, on the other hand, would furnish the necessary element. This would, of course, make it requisite that cabinet officers should be able to look after themselves on their feet. They would have to know their Department and be ready to answer such questions as are put to cabinet officers on the floor of Parliament.

President Wilson has inaugurated the policy of delivering his message to Congress personally. I think that is a good innovation. A Democrat could have made it, not a Republican. Washington had to go to Congress, so had Adams, but when Jefferson came in he said, "No, that is monarchical, and I will just write a letter to Congress," and so he did. Washington went once to the Senate and attempted to have the Senate concur with him in a treaty with the Indians. He took with him General Knox, who had frequently dealt with Indians. John Quincy Adams, in his diary, describes what happened as he learned it from a member of the Senate at that time. He says that in the conference, Washington found that every member of the Senate thought he knew more about the Indian treaty than General Knox. Whereupon, he, the father of our country, who has been represented as a model in every way, proved that he was no such "sissy" as some of his historians would like to make him out. His character was one which develops into grand proportions when you study it, but he was no mere steel engraving of copy-book perfection. When he got through with that particular session, he turned to Knox as he went out, and said he would be damned if he would come to the Senate again. Now I do not approve of profanity generally, but somehow or other I rather like that story because it lets in a little light on Washington and shows he was a man with good red blood.

The first power of the President that I wish to consider is the veto power. The English King has it, but never exercises it, i.e., he has not exercised it for two hundred years. If he attempted to exercise it under the present British Constitution, he would shake the throne and should he try it a second time he might not have a throne under him. The President, however, has the veto power under a provision of the Constitution. When he decides to differ with both Houses, certain members of demagogic tendency rise to say that the President is exercising a royal prerogative power, or that he is going back to the time of Imperial Rome. This might frighten an inexperienced man, but in reality it is mere bluster. As a matter of fact, the President represents the people in a much wider sense than any particular Congressional orator, for he was elected by all the people, while the Congressman was chosen by only one district. The Constitution says that if he disapproves of an act, he shall send it back with his objections and it enjoins upon him the duty of examining every act and every bill that comes to him, to see whether it ought to pass. He vetoes, therefore, in his representative capacity, with legislative and suspensive, but not absolute, power. A vetoed act is returned to the House, and if its supporters can succeed in getting a two-thirds majority in each House, the bill can still pass over his veto. This rarely happens, however, for the President can usually give reasons good enough to command the vote of at least the one-third of one House that is necessary to sustain his veto.

The second great control exercised by the President is that of Commander-in-Chief. This includes, first of all, his command over the army, which is complete. He can send the army where he chooses and he can call out the state militia to repel invasion, to suppress insurrection and to execute the laws, if the army or militia be necessary. Of that he alone is the judge. Early in our history certain state judges thought that the commander of the militia in each state should pass on the question as to whether an emergency had arisen which would justify the President in calling out the militia, but that was one hundred years ago.

To illustrate our practice now in regard to the execution of laws with the aid of the army, there is one very striking instance which occurred within my memory. Debs organized the American Railway Union in order to take the American people by the throat and say to them: "You shall not have any milk for your babies, you shall not have any food, you shall not have anything. I am going to stop every railroad in the country until you come with me and make Pullman pay his men what I think they ought to have, and what they think they ought to have." That was a secondary boycott, which Mr. Cleveland said ought to be suppressed. Since it involved the stoppage of mails and interstate commerce, the United States courts issued injunctions to prevent the malcontents from continuing their work of obstruction. When Debs's Union defied the court injunction, the President sent General Miles out to Chicago with a military force to suppress that obstruction to the United States laws.

At this Governor Altgeld protested. "I can

take care of this; I have not asked you to bring these men in here. Under the Constitution it is necessary for the governor or legislature to request the President to send troops in to suppress domestic insurrection which the governor of the state cannot control.''

To which Mr. Cleveland and Mr. Olney answered: ''That is true where the insurrection does not relate to the United States laws, but where there is an obstruction of the United States laws, the Supreme Court has decided repeatedly that the President is dealing, not with state territory, but with the territory of the United States. He can execute the laws of the United States on every foot of United States soil and have the whole army enforce them.'' And so he did.

Another indirect power of the President as Commander-in-Chief was exhibited in a most remarkable way during the Spanish War. We took over successively Cuba, Porto Rico and the Philippines, but for three years after we had annexed the Philippines, Congress took no action in regard to any of them. They formed territory ceded to us by virtue of the Treaty of Paris and Congress thought the Philippines were a poker that was a little bit hot for it to handle. The responsibility for them, therefore, fell upon the President, and as Commander-in-Chief he introduced a quasi-civil government, appointing a civil governor and commission, whom he authorized to pass laws—subject to veto of the Secretary of War—and to enforce them. He thus carried on a complete government in Porto Rico, Cuba and the Philippines under his power as Commander-in-Chief until Congress became sufficiently advised to enact needed legislation for their government. Cuba was turned over to her people, a Republic was set going. Then after several years, circumstances made it necessary for us to step in and take Cuba again. They had gotten into a row, as they frequently do in those Latin-American countries, and they were having a revolution.

When we first let Cuba go, we made what was called the Platt Amendment to the Cuban Treaty, suggested by Senator Platt of this state. That amendment provided for the restoration of order by the United States whenever law and order were disturbed and whenever life, liberty and property were not secure. Mr. Roosevelt, therefore, sent me down to Cuba with Mr. Bacon to see if we could not adjust the matter. When we arrived, we found twenty thousand revolutionist troops outside the city of Havana. President Palma had been so certain of peace that he had made no provision to suppress insurrections, and these troops were just about ready to march into Havana when I got there. I went out to stay at the house of the American Minister in a suburb just between the lines, and we did what we could to compose the situation. In those countries when they have a revolution, the first thing they do is to elect generals. The next thing they do is to determine what the uniform of the generals shall be, and then they get the guns and last of all they organize. President Palma became discouraged and resigned so that I had to proclaim myself Provisional Governor of Cuba. The Platt Amendment said that the United States could go into Cuba to preserve order; but the question was whether the President had the authority to go in without authorization by a resolution of Congress. I always thought that he had and Congress seemed to agree to it. So we went in, established a provisional government, passed a good election law, held an election and, at the end of a year, turned back the government to the Cubans, where it now is.

The President has not the power to declare war. Congress has that power; but if a foreign nation invades our country, the President must, without awaiting such declaration, resist and use the army and navy for that purpose. It is, therefore, possible for us to actually get into war before Congress makes a formal declaration. That is what happened in the Civil War. The Southern states seceded and Mr. Lincoln had war on his hands before Congress could declare it. The President thereupon declared a blockade of the Southern ports and the question then came up as to whether it was a legal blockade so that prizes might be taken as in a naval war. Our war vessels had captured merchant vessels trying to run the blockade, had taken them into prize courts, and had sold them there, distributing the proceeds among themselves. The owners fought the proceedings and these suits, called "The Prize Cases," were carried to the Supreme Court of the United States. The court held that while Congress under the Constitution had sole power to declare war, nevertheless, actual war might follow with all its legal consequences if a nation invaded our country or if such an insurrection arose as that which had just taken place in the Civil War.

Let me give you an example of presidential authority exercised in pursuance of his constitutional duty to execute the laws even when Congress passes no law on the subject-matter. The Canal Zone was acquired by a treaty with Panama that followed its recognition—a recognition made with such promptness that it has since attracted some criticism. Congress passed a law that the President should have power to govern that country for a year, but failed to renew the grant of power. The question arose then as to what was to be done in the Canal Zone. A prior act covering the building of the Panama Canal required the President to build it through a commission, but that was all. He might build it anywhere, either in Nicaragua or Panama, but he had no express governmental power over the Canal territory. He had, however, to see that the laws were executed, which meant that he must look after every piece of territory belonging to the United States and safeguard it in the interest of the people. It seemed to us, therefore, to be within the executive authority, until Congress should act, to continue the government of the Zone, maintain courts, execute men who committed murder, and discharge all the political functions required to constitute a law-abiding community.

Let me give you another instance of the President's exercising a law that Congress did not pass. Sarah Althea Hill thought she was married to Senator Sharon, at least she said she thought so. Senator Sharon was a rich man. She wished to share it. So she brought in the State courts of California a suit for divorce and alimony against the senator and exhibited a letter purporting to have been written by the senator admitting the marriage. She got into a great deal of litigation and employed as her lawyer Judge Terry. Senator Sharon then brought suit in the United States Court in California to have this

letter declared a forgery and delivered up to
him. Justice Field of the United States Supreme
Court heard the case on the circuit. Judge Terry,
who had been on the Supreme Court of California
in its early days and had served on the same
court with Judge Stephen J. Field, was a noted
duelist and was known to have killed one man
in a duel. Mr. Justice Field had been appointed
from the California court to be a Supreme Justice
of the United States by Mr. Lincoln during the
war. Pending the litigation, Senator Sharon died
and soon thereafter the association of Miss Hill
and Judge Terry as client and counsel developed
into a warmer relation and they became man and
wife. She was a very violent woman, as Judge
Terry was a violent man, and made threatening
demonstrations in court when Justice Field gave
the judgment against her. Justice Field sentenced
Mrs. Terry to thirty days' imprisonment for contempt because in her fury she insulted the Court
and attempted to commit violence upon the Judge.
The bitterness of feeling between the Terrys and
Justice Field was really heightened by the old
association between Judge Terry and Justice
Field as judicial colleagues. The Terrys frequently declared their intention, when occasion
offered, to kill Judge Field. Word of this came
to the Attorney-General, then W. H. H. Miller,
in Mr. Harrison's administration. He notified

the United States Marshal to direct a deputy to follow Justice Field in his Circuit work and protect him against any threatened attack.

As Justice Field was proceeding north from Los Angeles to San Francisco to hold court there, he got out for breakfast at Fresno. Unfortunately the Terrys reached the same station on another train at the same time. Justice Field and Neagle, the deputy marshal, got out of the train, went into the restaurant and sat down. When Judge and Mrs. Terry came in and Mrs. Terry saw Justice Field, she ran out to the car to get a revolver she had left in her satchel by an oversight. In the meantime Judge Terry went up to Justice Field, denounced him and struck him from behind. Thereupon Neagle arose, saying, "I am an officer, keep off," but Judge Terry continued to assault Justice Field. Neagle said he thought Judge Terry reached for a knife. At any rate, Neagle shot, and Terry fell dead at the feet of Justice Field.

Neagle was at once indicted by a state jury for murder. He went into the Federal Court and got a writ of *habeas corpus,* asking to be released on the ground that he was discharging a duty under the government of the United States. Judge Sawyer granted the writ and released Neagle. The state of California took the case to the Supreme Court of the United States. The court divided, with the Chief Justice and Justice Lamar dissenting. The majority of the court held, Mr. Justice Miller pronouncing the judgment, that the President was justified by the duty imposed upon him by the Constitution to see that the laws were faithfully executed. Although there was no specific law on the statute book conferring upon the President authority to direct Neagle to take the action he did, there was an implied obligation on the part of the government to protect its judges in discharging their duty from the violence of disappointed litigants, and this obligation was a law which it was the duty of the President to see executed. The President, therefore, has the right through his Attorney-General, who is the finger of his hand, to direct an officer of the United States to protect to the uttermost a justice while on judicial duty, even if it necessitates killing an assailant.

I cannot tell you all the officers of the United States—internal revenue men, customs men, post-office men, immigrant inspectors, public land men, reclamation men, marine hospital men—certainly 150,000 in number, who are subject to the direction of the President. In the executive work under this head, he wields a most far-reaching power in the interpretation of Congressional acts. A great many statutes never come before the court. The President or his officers for him have finally to decide what a statute means when it directs them to do something. Many statutes contain a provision that under that statute, regulations must be made by executive officers in order to facilitate their enforcement. This is quasi-legislative work. The situation in regard to the present income tax illustrates the necessity for regulations. You will recognize that regulations adopted by the President and his subordinates are sometimes necessary to straighten out law. If you desire to study a maze or look into a labyrinth, I commend you to the present income tax law.

Then often Congress relies upon the discretion of the President to accomplish such tremendous things as in the Panama Canal. It directed the President to build the Canal. It remained for him to appoint all the persons engaged in the work, and he became responsible for every one of them. Another notable instance of the reliance of Congress upon the President occurred in the Spanish War, when it appropriated $50,000,000 to be allotted at his discretion.

Yet it seems to me that a curtailment of the small duties now imposed on the President might well be made. The number of his appointments, for instance, might well be lessened. The President ought, of course, to appoint his Cabinet, the Supreme Court, ambassadors, ministers, generals and admirals, but beyond that I think appointments ought to be made without bothering the President about them. We have introduced a Civil Service reform system with a Civil Service Commission, and I trust that the matter of taking these subordinate officers out of politics will be pressed generally as a much-needed reform.

Is the position occupied by a postmaster of sufficient importance to justify the President in bothering with his appointment when he has such a problem as the Mexican situation on his hands? We are coming to the time when there are great complicated duties to perform under the government. We have departed from the Jefferson view, and we now think that the government can do a great many things helpfully, provided it has experts to do them. Is it not entitled to the best men to do these things? Yet how are experts obtainable unless they are selected to permanent positions by those who are looking for experts and not looking for men who exercise influence at the polls?

I recommended to Congress four times, that is, in each annual message, that it enable me to put these men under the Civil Service law and in the classified service; but it did not do it, and why? Because all local officers now have to be confirmed by the Senate. That power of confirmation gives a hold on the Executive and each

Senator and each Congressman wants to name the postmaster and the other local officers in his district or state. The consequence is that Congressmen do not wish the Senate to lose the power of confirmation. They believe this personal patronage to be a means of perpetuating their own tenure. As a matter of fact, this is not the case. Few men help themselves politically in the long run through the use of patronage. It is a boomerang. Some few manage to make it useful, but generally when a man secures an appointment for a henchman, as the saying is in Washington— and it is a very true one—he makes one ingrate and twenty enemies. The result is that after he has served a term or two, he begins to find those aspiring constituents, whom he did not appoint, rising like snakeheads to strike him down.

Therefore, if Congressmen really had wisdom and looked ahead, they would rid themselves of responsibility for these appointments, would abolish the necessity for confirmation by the Senate, and would thus enable the President to classify them under the Civil Service law and merit system. But we have made progress and I am not discouraged about it. Ultimately we shall get the Senate to consent to give up that power, though at present the Democratic majority in the two Houses is fierce against such a suggestion, and quite naturally so, for, while the

Republican party has been in control for sixteen years, the trend into office has been Republican and the Democrats wish to change it. That is human nature, and I am merely regretting, not condemning it. Perhaps if the Republicans come back into power after four years, they will not be quite so hungry as the Democrats were after sixteen years of famine, and we may have a little less wolfish desire to get at the offices.

The time taken up in the consideration of minor appointments by executive officers, the President and Cabinet officers especially, is a great waste and no one can know the nervous vitality that can be expended upon them until he has had actual experience.

Of course they lead to some amusing experiences, for there is nothing which gives such a chance for the play of human impulse as office-seeking. I remember having a lady come into my office when I was Secretary of War. Her boy had passed the examination for West Point, but a medical board had examined him and found that his chest did not measure enough for his height. She came in to urge me to waive that defect. I explained to her the necessity for great care in the appointment of army officers, because if, after being commissioned, they had any organic trouble, they were disqualified for further discharge of their duty, and would be retired on three-fourths pay without rendering any real service to the government. She listened with gloom to my explanation, and asked me to look at the papers. I took them in her presence and went through them. I found that the young man had, on the basis of 100, made 93 per cent in all his mental examinations. That isn't done by every candidate for West Point, and there is no reason why we should not have brains as well as brawn in army officers. So I looked again at the measurements and concluded he was a man we ought not to lose. I told her: "Madam, I did not have so much difficulty in filling out my chest measurement. Your boy shows such general intelligence that I have no doubt he will have sense enough to pursue a regimen that will make him sufficiently enlarge his chest measurement, so I am going to waive the objection and let him in." She had not expected so quick a decision in her favor, and was taken back a little. She hesitated a minute, and then, with an angelic smile, she said to me, "Mr. Secretary, you are not nearly so fat as they say you are."

Then I had another experience. A lady in Washington, whose husband had some political influence, came and labored with me for six weeks or more to appoint her son to a position. She secured the aid of Senators and Congressmen in formidable number and came with them to see that they spoke with emphasis. The place was one requiring technical qualification, and following the recommendation of the head of the Bureau, I appointed somebody else. I then received a letter from the mother, saying that I was most ungrateful, since I declined to make her a happy woman as I could have done by a turn of my hand. She complained further that she had labored with her state delegation and got all the votes for an administration bill in which I was especially interested and this was the way I had rewarded her.

When you get a letter like that, the first thing you do is to think how you can be severe with a person who has committed an impropriety, or even been a little impertinent. Then you may compose an answer. Then if you are wise, you will put the letter in a drawer and lock the drawer. Take it out in the course of two days—such communications will always bear two days' delay in answering—and when you take it out after that interval, you will not send it. That is just the course I took. After that, I sat down and wrote her just as polite a letter as I could, telling her I realized a mother's disappointment under such circumstances, but that really the appointment was not left to my mere personal preference, that I had to select a man with technical qualifications, and had, therefore, to follow the recommendation of the head of the Bureau. I expressed the hope that her son would go on to accomplish what she had hoped for him in the position which he then had. That mollified her and she wrote me a note saying she was sorry she had written as she had.

But the appointment I sent in was not confirmed at once and after an interval I received a letter which purported to come from her husband, though it was in the same handwriting as all the others. I was therein advised that, due to the nervous prostration that had followed her disappointment in this case, she had to take to her bed and had developed a most serious case of cancer of the stomach. Would I not restore her to health by withdrawing the first name and replacing it by her son's? I had to write another letter, this one to the husband, to say that I hoped the diagnosis would prove to be inaccurate, that I sympathized with him in the sorrow he must have in the serious illness of his wife, but that it was impossible to withdraw the name sent in. The man whom I appointed was confirmed, and within two days after I received that letter, we gave a musicale at the White House. The first two people to greet Mrs. Taft and me were this husband and wife, though the wife had so recently been *in articulo mortis*.

Another great power of the President is his control of our foreign relations. In domestic matters, the Federal government shares every field, executive, judicial and legislative, with the states, but in foreign affairs, the whole governmental control is with the President, the Senate and Congress. The states have nothing to do with it. The President initiates a treaty and the Senate confirms it. The Senate, however, cannot initiate a treaty, the President alone can do that. Congress' powers to declare war and regulate our foreign commerce are its chief powers in respect to our foreign relations. So that, except in ratifying treaties, in regulating commerce and in declaring war, the President guides our whole foreign policy.

Through the State Department he conducts all negotiation and correspondence with other governments and according to the Constitution he receives ambassadors and foreign ministers. Now you might possibly think that that meant only that he must have a flunky at the White House to take their cards—but it means a good deal more. He appoints ambassadors and ministers to other countries and instructs them. He receives the diplomatic representatives from other countries and does business with them. He construes treaties and asserts the rights of our government and our citizens under them. He considers and decides the rights of other governments and their subjects in a way which practically binds our government and people. And in order to receive ambassadors and ministers, he must determine whether they have been properly accredited, so that they have the proper authority to act for the country they claim to represent.

When there is a dispute as to what person is the chief executive of a foreign country and therefore entitled to send an ambassador or minister, the President must decide it. In other words, he alone can exercise the power of recognition. How important a power this is, we may know from our recent experiences with Mexico, for President Wilson, by withholding recognition from General Huerta, was able to render his longer tenure as chief executive impossible.

In our foreign relations it is often the President's duty to formulate the national claim of sovereignty over territory whose ownership is in dispute. This is a political question and his decision or claim in regard to it is taken as final by the Supreme Court.

In the Fur-Seal Controversy, Mr. Blaine took the position that our jurisdiction reached out over the Bering Sea. The question was contested in the Supreme Court by the British and the Canadian governments. The Supreme Court said: "We cannot determine this. It is a political question and must, therefore, be decided by the President through his Secretary of State." We then submitted the issue to an international tribunal, and the decision was against us.

Another great power of the President is the power of pardons and reprieves. This is not to be determined by rules of law nor indeed by absolute rules of any kind and must, therefore, be wielded skilfully lest it destroy the prestige and supremacy of law. Sometimes one is deceived. I was. Two men were brought before me, both of whom were represented as dying. When a convict is near his end, it has been the custom to send him home to die. So, after having all the surgeons in the War Department examine them to see that the statements made to me about them were correct, I exercised the pardoning power in their favor. Well, one of them kept his contract and died, but the other seems to be one of the healthiest men in the community today.

The President is also the titular head of a party and ought to have a large influence in legislation. He is made responsible to the country for his party's majority in Congress, and does thereby have some voice in legislation. Some Presidents have more control than others, but all Presidents find as the patronage is distributed, and as the term goes on, that the influence and power that they have over legislation rapidly diminishes. In fact, when there are no more offices to distribute and somebody else comes into view as the next

President, the authority of the incumbent becomes strictly limited to his constitutional functions. All of this tends to show that a President who seeks legislative changes and reforms should begin early.

The people think that the Presidency gives a man an opportunity to make a lot of personal appointments. I can recall some of these personal appointments, but I tell you they are very few. There are certain political obligations involving the recognition of party leaders which he has to take into consideration with reference to some appointments. But when it comes to purely personal appointments, one can count them on the fingers of one hand. It is well that it is so. A President with his proper sense of duty finds many men in office whom he ought to let continue and the question of friendship for others can play no part in displacing them.

The social influence of the President in Washington is not much. I think perhaps it might be useful if it were a little more, for the question of precedence, which makes everybody outside of Washington laugh, sometimes becomes a very serious matter. As the French ambassador once said, when there are three hundred people, they cannot all go through the door at one time. Somebody has to go first, therefore it is most important to fix who that somebody shall be. But nobody in Washington has the authority to say. If only the army and navy were concerned, the matter would be easy enough, because they are controlled by the President and he can issue orders that they must respect, but with civil officers he has no such authority. Congress could, of course, provide rules of social and official precedence, either by legislation or executive order, as is done in all European countries. But here such a proposal would be laughed out of Congressional halls, though it would be a wise measure to prevent confusion, unnecessary friction and heartburning.

The very men who make most fun of such matters and profess to despise their consideration are in actual practice the most unreasonable as to their own places at functions. The House of Representatives is supposed to be the embodiment of democracy and contempt for social distinctions, yet of all the people in the world who have made a fuss over the matter of precedence, speakers of the House of Representatives have been the most insistent on their proper place at official dinners. The speaker says: "I represent the body of the people who come from the soil and the people who make this country. Therefore, I decline to sit after the presiding officer of the Senate." An ambassador says: "I am the personal representative of my sovereign. If he were here in

Washington, he would sit next to the President."
The Cabinet officer says: "The President is the
head. I am connected with him as Secretary of
War, the Cabinet is a small body and the Senate
is a large body. Therefore, we are bigger men
than the Senate and we ought to have precedence." In fact, the head of a scientific bureau
came in to see me one day and said, "I think you
ought to put me after the Supreme Court." He
even filed a brief with me on the subject, to the
effect that "I run an independent department.
The judges represent the judicial branch, and the
President the executive branch, and the heads of
the two Houses, the legislative branch, while I
represent the scientific branch." Indeed, the
matter of procedure is not such a joke as it seems
outside. It is not so important as to who comes
first as that their order of precedence should be
once determined.

The President is made responsible for everything, especially for hard times. Of course his
supporters claim credit for good crops, so that
perhaps it is not so unfair to charge him with
responsibility for bad crops and for everything
else that happens wrong during his term. Every
President strives to do the best he can for the
country. It is a great task, one of the heaviest
in the world. A man does not really know, until
he gets out of the office, what the strain is. And,

therefore, knowing that he is struggling to do the best he can, while he may differ with you, while he may do things that seem to you absurd, consider that he is there, elected by the American people, as your representative, and remember that while he is in office he is entitled to your respect. Now, don't be flippant in regard to him. Don't think it shows you to be a big man to criticise him or speak contemptuously of him. You may differ with his policy, but always maintain a profound respect for a man who represents the majesty and the sovereignty of the American people.

CHAPTER IV

THE SIGNS OF THE TIMES

WE are living at a time when political and social conditions are a bit chaotic, and it is a little difficult to distinguish between the symptoms that are ephemeral and those which are permanent. What we must do is to try to make things better and to save from the past the things which are good. It is often true that a movement that is excessive and destructive in one way, ends by being the basis of great progress after reaction from its excesses has left what is valuable in it.

Our American Revolution, which we are accustomed to regard as quite important—and it was for us—did not really represent a great world change such as was represented in the French Revolution. It grew out of a very unwise, selfish colonial policy on the part of Great Britain. We were right and wise in putting it through, and our ancestors demonstrated great courage and great tenacity in fighting it. It certainly gave us independence and an opportunity for expansion that we should not otherwise have had. But the pap that we have been brought up on with respect to the tremendous outrages which Great Britain inflicted on us was sweetened a little bit. If you would see the other side, read Trevelyan's "American Revolution." In this you will see that while the right was certainly with us, we were not quite so much outraged as it seemed in our earlier childhood studies. The American Revolution did as much good for England as it did for us, because it taught her proper colonial policy, and today the colonial policy of Great Britain is one of the greatest instances of statesmanship in history. In her dealing with Canada, with Australia and with the South African Republic, she has given them such self-government that, far from wishing to sever the bond with the mother country, they cherish it.

The French Revolution indicated a very much more important movement among peoples. It developed awful excesses. The wild declarations and extremes practiced by the Committee of Safety in the French Revolution were revolting to any man affected by ordinary humane considerations and had in fact a remarkable effect in strengthening conservatism in England. Indeed, they caused the issue and the bitter personal quarrel between the one-time warm associates, Burke and Fox. The natural result of those excesses was to be expected. It took the shape of the man on horseback. The imperial control of

Napoleon led the French people into a military waste of strength which has affected the French race even down to the present time. Yet Napoleon, by building up his Code Napoleon, and by spreading over Europe the idea that the people were the basis of government, profoundly affected political conceptions and conditions. There followed a reaction in the Holy Alliance, which was a combination to maintain the Divine Right of Kings, and then the spirit of the French Revolution reasserted itself in 1830. In fact from then on until now the movement toward more and more popular government has gone on continuously in France, Germany, Austria and elsewhere. It is spreading today even more widely than it ever did before, and every country, even Russia, has to count the cost with respect to the will of the people.

When I went through Russia after the Russian-Japanese War, I met one of the leading diplomats of that country who greeted me with, "Well, how do you like it?" "How do I like what?" I asked. "How do you like helping Japan to lick Russia?" Those were the homely expressions that he used. To which I replied, "We did not help Japan to lick Russia." "But," he said, "you did in effect. Your people and your press sympathized and they expressed the kindly sympathy that counts for so much at such a time." "The government cannot control our people," I responded. "They think for themselves and express themselves as they see fit. We cannot control the press in our country, but we have observed all the laws of neutrality with respect to the war, and if some of the people expressed themselves in favor of Japan, it was only because they were in favor of the under dog in the fight." "Why did you give up?" I inquired further; "You were getting stronger and stronger." "Yes," he said, "we had to fight at the end of a 5,000-mile, single-track railway, but handicapped as we were, we got our forces out there ready to fight and we could have gone in and beaten the Japanese." "Why didn't you?" I asked. "Why did you make peace?" "The trouble is," he explained, "we were living on a volcano at home. Our people were opposed to the war, and we did not go on, lest the throne would be a forfeit." This is only an indication that even in the country that is supposed to represent the most absolute of empires, the people are manifesting a control. The Douma was given too much power at first, so that universal suffrage was necessarily a failure in the condition of the people at that time. But the Douma now is gradually acquiring useful power and in the course of the next twenty-five or fifty years Russia will probably have a popular constitutional government.

We have had democracy in this country for one hundred and twenty-five years, or indeed for two hundred and twenty-five years. It is now proposed to have more democracy to supply the present defects of our existing democracy. This is one phase of the present situation that I wish to discuss. Another is the spread of the fraternal spirit, the desire of one to help another, the actual improvement and increase in the brotherhood of man which we are seeing in society, and a third is trades-unionism, its essence and what is to be hoped for or feared from it.

If you will read a book like Chamberlain on "The Foundations of the Nineteenth Century," especially the preface, which is written by a man who uses a better style than Chamberlain, you will find that he attempts to summarize the progress of the previous eighteen centuries as a predicate for the strides of human civilization in the nineteenth. As he minimizes the effect of one century and then another, you note how few centuries, in his judgment, play any part in the onward march, and you are discouraged as to what one man can do to help along any movement that shall really be world-wide or permanent.

The effect is much the same upon your personal hope of accomplishing some good in the world as when a professor of astronomy takes you over to the observatory, lets you look through the telescope, tells you that light takes something like eight minutes to come the 95,000,000 miles from the sun to the earth, and then says that the sun after all is a pretty poor thing considered in connection with what other suns there are. When you find furthermore that some stars are so far distant that the light you are now receiving on your retina started from them centuries ago, you say to yourself: "Well, what's the use? If we are such atoms and so unimportant in the general result, what's the use?"

Still if you study Chamberlain's history of the eighteen centuries you will find that, after all, the men who were real factors in the world civilization were the geniuses who were able to interpret and enforce what was inchoate in the minds of all but had no definite expression and led to no useful action. Each atom counts something, two make a molecule and the world is made up of them—at least it was in my college days. Therefore, what we are here for is to make the best possible effort to help along the general weal, and it is no excuse, because we cannot play a large part, that we should play no part at all and should feel no sense of responsibility for what we can do.

What then of conditions of civilization in our country in the last half-century? The Civil War grew out of a great moral and social issue. It was a moral issue on the part of the North and

a social issue on the part of the South. Material
considerations were subordinated. After the war
we had a pretty hard time in getting over its
immediate effects. The panic of 1873, which
prostrated all business, was the result of the
excesses of the war, the overissue of legal tender
and the feverish, unhealthy expansion that followed. In 1878, we resumed specie payments.
I presume no country in the world ever showed
such an enormous expansion and such material
growth as ours between 1878 and 1907. It was
shown in the useful inventions. Steam had been
invented before, but it was increased in its uses,
and electricity was made the tool of man. Now
it is easy to follow that kind of material expansion. We can count the growth in wealth and
trace the effect of it on the people, for they all
got into the chase for the dollar.

In the West, the pioneer spirit was so strong
that they were glad to have anything in the way
of development at any cost. Counties would issue
railroad bonds to build railroads and would give
the bonds to the railroads. They would give
franchises of all sorts and do everything that
they thought would help open the country. There
was a most substantial increase in the average
income, and the average comfort, especially in
the bodily comfort, of everyone. Have you ever
thought that today the humblest workman has

more bodily comfort in many ways than Queen
Elizabeth or even George III? We had learned
the advantage of combination in machinery and
we adopted it in business.

This brought about great combinations of plant
and capital which reduced the cost of producing
commodities necessary to man to a price never
conceived of before. I do not wish to depreciate
the value or importance of improvement in
material comfort. When you hear a man denounce
it, you may know that either he is not a clear,
calm thinker, or else he is a demagogue. Material
growth and material comfort are essential for
the development of mental and spiritual activities.
The result of this combination and material
expansion, however, was to create great corporations which began to get control of things. The
same spirit of combination entered into politics
and we had machines and bosses which lent their
hand to, and furnished a complacent instrument
for, corporations. Time was when they ordered
delegates in a convention with the same degree of
certainty that the order would be supplied, as they
did steel rails or any other commodity. That
time has passed and why? Because the danger
of plutocracy forced itself on the people. Leaders
took it up and showed it to them; and in
the last ten years we have had a great movement to eliminate corporate and money control

in politics. Great statutes have been passed—the anti-trust law, the interstate commerce law, the statutes against the use of contributions from corporations in politics, the statutes requiring the showing of the electoral expenses, have all been brought about in response to a popular demand.

The people failed to scrutinize before, but now that they are aroused and have taken matters in their own hands, they have brought about reform. The fact that he is supported by bosses is now generally enough to defeat a man, and the charge that he has a machine with him is enough to interfere with his electoral success. Organization is necessary for political success; even reformers find that out after they get into politics, but today there is an unreasonable prejudice against it. The great and good effect of the reform, however, is that corporations are no longer in politics. Of course corruption is not all gone, but it is largely stayed, and there is no longer any chance that corporations can control as they did.

But the leviathan of the people cannot be aroused in this way and his movement stopped at the median line. We must expect unwise excess. Sincere reformers have reasoned that because we had the representative form of government during this corrupt period, it is the representative form of government which is responsible. Because we had courts during the corrupt period, the courts are responsible for the corruption. Therefore we must change the representative system by injecting more democracy into it and we must change the courts by injecting more democracy into them and require the people at an election to decide cases instead of judges on the Bench. These are the excesses to which we trend.

We are a pretty great people. We admit it. We have great confidence in what we can do, and when we are set, neither an economic law drawn from political science nor experience seems a very formidable objection. We are a successful people in machinery, and so we take our analogy for political reforms from machinery. We found that by uniting various mechanical elements we could make machines which would do as much as one hundred or one thousand men in the same time. So we think that if we are only acute enough to devise a governmental machine which will work without effort on the part of the people, we can sit at home while elections run themselves so well that only what the good people desire in political action will necessarily result. We want the equivalent of what, in the slang of practical mechanics, we call a fool-proof machine, because anybody can run it and no fool can interfere with its normal operation. So these political reformers are hunting a corrupt-politician-proof machine for government. It does not and cannot exist. No government can exist which does not depend upon the activity, the honesty and the intelligence of those who form it. The initiative, the referendum and the recall have been urged and in many states adopted, as a machine which no boss or corrupt politician can prevent from producing honest, effective political results. They are expected to reform everything and those who doubt their wisdom are, for the time being, in the minds of many enthusiasts, public enemies.

The representative system, on the contrary, recognizes that government, in the actual execution of governmental measures, and in the actual detailed preparation of governmental measures, is an expert matter. To attempt to devise and adopt detailed legislative measures to accomplish the general purpose of the people through a mass vote at a popular election is just as absurd as it would be for all those present at a town meeting to say, "We will all of us now go out and build a bridge, or we will use a theodolite." Thus to say that by injecting more democracy you can cure the defects of our present democracy is to express one of those epigrams that, like many of its kind, is either not true at all or is only partly true and is even more deceptive than if it were wholly untrue.

Take the power of appointment in executive work. You elect officers, choosing men of character, intelligence, and experience for a few great offices, and then what do you do under the Federal Constitution? You turn over to the President the appointment of great officers because he needs intelligence, knowledge and skill to make their selections.

Consider the system of general direct primaries in the selection of judges. There is a ticket at the primaries on which something like twenty or thirty lawyers run for the Supreme Bench. Some of them go around and tell the electors how they will decide on questions after they get in. The qualifications of most of them as lawyers and as men are not known to the people. Some of them are prominent because they have been in the head-lines of newspapers as figuring in sensational cases. Others have political prominence but no public experience to test their judicial capacity. Do you think this method of selection by the people would lead to the choice of a learned, skilled lawyer with that experience, courage and fine judicial quality that are to make him a great judge? Of course it would not. It has been my duty to select more judges in a term of four years than any other President, and I have had to look into and compare the results of selection of judicial candidates by popular general primary and by convention, so that I know what I am talking about when I say that the primary system has greatly injured the average capacity of our elective judiciary.

Why should we not use common sense in matters of government just as we use common sense in our own business? Why should we be afraid to tell the people that they are not fitted to select high judicial officers? They are not. You know you are not. You could not tell me who would be good judges for Connecticut, or for any state in the Union where you happen to live unless you went about and investigated the matter. If you are put in a position of responsibility, you have sense enough to know where to find out the facts and then to make the selection, but the people lack that opportunity. So how is the question to be solved? By electing a Chief Executive and charging him with the responsibility of selecting competent men to act as judges. That is what is meant by the short ballot.

Reformers-for-politics-only include as many vote-getting planks in a platform as they can get in it without regard to their consistency or inconsistency. They sometimes combine the short ballot with the initiative, referendum and recall though they are utterly at variance. The referendum is the submission of every issue to the people.

The short ballot, on the contrary, means putting up one or two men whose names shall not encumber the ballot. Have you ever seen these ballots? They are a yard long and a yard wide. They have a hundred and twenty names on them and the people are expected to make a selection. They are to make a selection of ten out of fifty or one hundred names. Why, it would seem to be mathematically demonstrable that that is absurd. But when some men get into politics and talk about the people, it seems as if they had to abandon ordinary logic. I am just as much in favor of popular government as anybody, but I am in favor of popular government as a means to attain good government, not in order to go upon the stump and say, "Vote for me because I am in favor of the people. The people are all wise and never make a mistake."

Now what is the initiative? In practice, it means that if 5 per cent of the electorate can get together and agree on a measure, they shall compel all the rest of the electorate to vote as to whether it shall become law or not. There is no opportunity for amendment, or for discussion. The whole legislative program is put into one act to be voted on by the people. Speakers will get up and claim that the millennium will be brought about by some measure that they advocate. Suppose it is voted in? It never has had the test of discussion and amendment that every law ought to have. I am not complaining of the movement that brings about this initiative and referendum, for that is prompted by a desire to clinch the movement against corruption, on the theory that you cannot corrupt the whole people and that the initiative and referendum mean detailed and direct government by the whole people. But the theory is erroneous. The whole people will not vote at an election, much less at a primary. When the people are thus represented at the polls by a small minority there is nothing that the politicians will not be able to do with that minority when they get their hands in.

This is still a new movement, for which we have little precedent to guide us, but we have seen politicians fit their methods to any form of government. Their chance is always through the neglect to vote on the part of the majority of the electorate and this new system calls out fewer votes than ever.

Now what is the referendum? It is a reference of the thing proposed by the initiative to the people who are to vote on it. These reformers-for-politics-only are never content to acquire a majority of the electorate vote for the adoption of the measure referred. They seem to love the promotion of the power of the minority.

What answer do the people themselves give with reference to the wisdom of the referendum? At many elections candidates run at the same time that questions are referred to the people, and what is the usual result of the vote? In Oregon, where they have tried it most, and where the people are best trained, they do sometimes get as much as 70 per cent of those who vote on candidates to vote on the referendum; but generally, as in Colorado, the vote at the same election upon the referendum measures is not more than 50 per cent—sometimes as low as 25 or 20 per cent—of those who vote for candidates. Why, in New York they were voting as to whether they should have a constitutional convention, and how did the total referendum vote compare with the total electorate? It was just one-sixth of that total.

They have tried it in Switzerland. We get a good many of these new nostrums from that country. They said in Switzerland, "These men vote for candidates, they shall vote on referendums." What was the result? The electors went up to the polls and solemnly put in tickets. When they opened the ballots, they were blanks. What does that mean? It means that the people themselves believe that they do not know how to vote on those issues, and that such issues ought to be left to the agents whom they select as competent persons to discuss and pass upon them in accordance with the general principles that they have laid down in party platforms. In Oregon, at the last Presidential election, the people were invited to vote on thirty-one statutes, long, complicated statutes, and in order to inform them, a book of two hundred and fifty closely printed pages was published to tell them what the statutes meant.

I ask you, my friends, you who are studious, you who are earnest men who would like to be a part of the people in determining what their policy should be, I ask you to search yourselves and confess whether you would have the patience to go through that book of two hundred and fifty closely printed pages to find out what those acts meant? You would be in active business, you would go down to the polls and say, "What is up today?" You would be told: "Here are thirty-one statutes. Here are two hundred and fifty pages that we would like to have you read in order that you may determine how you are to vote on them." You would not do it.

There was once a Senator from Oregon named Jonathan Bourne, who advocated all this system of more democracy. He served one term in the Senate and then sent word back to his constituents that he was not coming home at the time of the primary. He said that he was not on trial, for a man who had worked as hard as he had for the people could not be on trial. Instead, he said, it was the people of Oregon who were on trial, to say whether they appreciated a service like his. They did not stand the test, and he was defeated at the primary. Then he concluded that after all he would have to forgive them and take pity on their blindness. So he went out to Oregon and ran on another ticket to give them the benefit of his service. But still they resisted the acid test. He himself went to the polls to vote at this election where there were thirty-one statutes to be approved or rejected. How many of the thirty-one submitted to him do you suppose he voted for? The newspapers reported him as admitting that he voted on just three, and the other twenty-eight he left to fate. Now, gentlemen, is not that a demonstration? Is not that a *reductio ad absurdum* for this system of pure and direct democracy?

CHAPTER V

MORE SIGNS OF THE TIMES

THE present movement for a purer and more direct democracy—the initiative, referendum and recall—is clearly an ineffective method of securing wise legislation, good official agents, or even a real expression of the people's will. The representative system is the most valuable system that has thus far been invented to make popular government possible and the introduction of more democracy, so-called, is a retrograde step. It is going back to the machinery of the New England town meeting and of the Republics of Greece and Rome, which we have given up because conditions have so changed as to make it impracticable and ineffective.

In the small number of people who constituted the town meeting in New England, or in a Greek city, it was possible to discharge the comparatively simple functions fulfilled by government because of the high average intelligence of the freemen who took part. But even the Greeks ran into difficulties, and if you will read Lord Acton, possibly the greatest historical authority on the subject, you will find that pure democracy, as it is called, resulted in disaster. We now have a much more complicated government and more democracy will not supply its needs.

The representative system, much abused as it is, is the system that has rescued us from plutocracy. Its laws are the laws that have done the work. Congress has adopted laws that have taken hold of the corporations, and Congress is the most perfect model of representative government. Why did Congress act? Because the people were aroused. You must have the people aroused in order to make any system effective, and when this is the case under the representative system, there is no difficulty about its working.

The general primary is, of course, a good thing for certain leading offices, but if you resort to it for selecting judges or subordinate officials whose qualifications the public cannot be supposed to know, the result will be anything but good. Men will be put into office by some fortuitous circumstance, such as a particular advertisement in the newspapers. Thus your Senator, and your governor, might well be elected by the general primary as the result of party selection, but if the people selected judges and subordinate officers they would have to take men without regard to their qualifications. The short ballot means, as I said, that the people should select leading officers who should in turn select the subordinate officers and appoint the judges.

To the objection that voters will not vote on referendums, it is urged that they ought to be compelled to do so. This is a futile remedy. Burke said you cannot bring an indictment against the people, and it is equally true that you cannot indict a great majority of the electorate for not complying with their electoral duties. Suppose you attempt to forfeit their right to vote, you may injure them, but you injure the whole people a great deal more. The 80 per cent of the population whose welfare is directly affected by the action of the electorate, but who are not by law permitted to vote, are entitled to have the more intelligent voters retained in the electorate. For, I am sorry to say, it is generally among the intelligent part of the community that we find neglect of electoral duties. The wisest course, therefore, is to give to the people as much electoral duty as they are ordinarily able and willing to perform, and no more. The fundamental fallacies in the initiative, referendum and recall are, first, that they impose on the voters three times the electoral work they had to do under the representative system, and second, that the additional work involved is of a kind that could be done much better through agents than by the people directly.

As to the recall of officers, I have only to say that if you elect a man for three years to try to help your city, or state, you must not make him subject to recall at any moment by those candidates or people whom he has had to disappoint in order to do his work effectively. Under the system of recall you are not going to secure the men who will work well by looking ahead to preserve the real public interest, but men who are trimmers, devoting their time to politics and doing as little as possible to avoid criticism. Your executive officers should be men of independence, courage and ability, who are interested in the public and willing to encounter criticism for the time being in order that they may carry out those policies that are going to inure to public benefit in the end. By making them subject to recall, you eliminate all independence and courage in your officers.

Another sign of recent times which will repay consideration has been aptly termed "muckraking." Mr. Roosevelt took the word from Bunyan's "Pilgrim's Progress" to describe the irresponsible and slanderous attacks upon public officials, which were made merely for the purpose of selling the wares of penny-a-liners. To eliminate corporations from politics and to bring them under government control, as I have described, it was doubtless necessary to formulate charges against individuals and political leaders and it was not to be expected that misstatements would not creep into such personal attacks. While many people were doubtless injured unjustly, it was essential that general corrupt conditions should be revealed to the public. But there were a great many who were induced to go into outrageous muckraking solely for profit, and magazines filled with such stuff and spreading real poison among the people were sent in the mails at a much less rate than it cost the government to carry them. I am glad to say muckraking is not so profitable now and it has been greatly reduced in volume.

But the opportunity for attacking prominent and powerful men in this way has served to create a condition that we still suffer from. It has brought about a feeling that nobody is to be trusted, and it has spread too far the idea that all men are corrupt. In fact, it has led to the feeling that everybody is on the same level in matters of character, learning, skill and effectiveness of labor, and, in short, that every man is as good as everybody else in everything. The idea is that men are on a dead level. There is no room for leadership in such a view. Inequality is essential to progress. If you make a dead level there will be no interest in life or motive for effort, and you will destroy the very spring of progress and the fountain of Christian civilization.

We now have political parties that are made by vertical divisions among the voters. In each party we have the intelligent and the fortunate, with those who are not so intelligent nor so experienced nor so well circumstanced. What will be the tendency of this refusal to recognize intelligence and high character in those who deserve it? It will make the parties horizontal layers in the body politic. It will unite in one party those who are ignorant and unfortunate, and array them against the intelligent and those who have the ability for leadership. When that comes about, the Republic will be in danger, because the permanence and usefulness of the Republic rests upon the controlling influence of men of intelligence, experience, patriotism and character. This array of a proletariat against intelligent and successful leadership produces factionalism in society. Factionalism is a class spirit which will sacrifice the interest of the whole to the interest of the class. It sometimes permeates a majority, but more frequently a minority. It is illustrated for us by the militancy of English women suffragists, who will sacrifice property, art and even life, in order to convince the majority that unless they receive the vote they will destroy all society.

We cannot, of course, yield to such a force.

Nor can we yield to trades-unionism when it seeks to promote so-called labor interests by lawless violence and dynamite. The bonds of society will be loosed if we do. I would not for a moment be thought to say that those who are in favor of more democracy, through the initiative and referendum, are factionalists, and insincere in their view that that system will work a good result in the fight against corruption in politics. I only think that they are idealists in this matter, and don't fully understand the practical operation of the system which they recommend.

In this movement against corruption in politics and corporate control, it was necessary that corporate control should be attacked. The muckraking added to it aroused a spirit against all success in business, whether the methods pursued were honest or not. The result has been a hysteria that prompts hostility to capital even when it is working in honest lines and earning an honest profit. In many states it has led to excessive restrictive legislation and has terrorized capital; it has shrunk investments and frightened those who have money until today there is lots of money in the banks everywhere but it can't be borrowed for any length of time because nobody will put it into permanent or active investment.

This state of affairs is likely to continue for some years. I am not complaining about it because it is part of what we had to pay for the great reform that was accomplished. After a while confidence will be restored, and we shall come to our senses, just as they did in Kansas in the Populist days. The Kansas farmers concluded that all their unhappiness, and they suffered real stress, was due to the wicked mortgagees who had lent them money on mortgage security and who insisted on the payment of interest and even the principal when it was due. So they elected a Populist legislature and passed a law providing that a mortgagee could not foreclose his mortgage under two years. They did this by stay laws and by requiring an obstructive procedure in collection of debts. As a result, capital fled the state as men would flee yellow fever. When there was no money at all left in the state and they found that they couldn't get any, they began to recognize the benefit in money loaned on mortgages. Their next legislature repealed all these laws and devoted its attention to advertising their change of attitude in Eastern markets where money could be had and mortgages could be floated, promising to be good thereafter, and in general welcoming the capitalists who would advance money on farms.

The next sign of the times is pleasanter to dwell upon, that is, the spread of the fraternal spirit that has grown out of this great material development. Material development in this country had grown into corruption, undue luxury and waste at the hands of men who did not realize the responsibility of having been fortunate in accumulating money, and this absorption in the chase for the dollar began to pall on the people. They tired of statistics of the growth of business, and began to look about for some justification for our activities. The change has brought a greater popular interest in the less fortunate who have fallen behind in the race.

This feeling has much weakened the influence of the *laissez faire* school of political and economic thought which was largely in control when I was in college. Professor Sumner was a strong member of this school. He was sure of his opinions and taught them. But we have now drifted away from some of his moorings, and today a good many professors are giving way to their imagination in suggesting remedies that have not stood the test of experience. Yet it is generally conceded that the government can do a lot to help the people that individual enterprise cannot do. We have also gone far in the matter of regulation, though there again we are likely to go to excesses.

It is quite probable that we shall find out by hard knocks that the government cannot perform everything now expected of it. Nevertheless, under the influence of a greater fraternal spirit, we have done a great deal. The housing statutes, the safety appliances both for passengers and employees, the restrictions on the hours of labor, the rules against child labor, the pure food law, the white slave law, the thorough health regulations, the control of public utilities, the growth in the public charitable institutions of the state, the parcels post and the rural delivery, all are instances of what the government has done to help the individual by applying the results of public taxation and restrictive laws. Moreover, we find among rich men a greater feeling of responsibility for their fortunes, which is proven by their large donations. Among those less wealthy we find an activity in philanthropic organizations and in work of a charitable character that has vastly increased during the last decade. In education, too, we have widened out, especially in vocational study, by preparing the pupils directly for wage earning by skilled labor.

Unfortunately, however, many good people in social settlements and in philanthropic work devote their attention so exclusively to the sore and rotten spots of society that they lose their sense of proportion, and bring hysteria even into this movement. Persons so affected come to think that if suffering, wickedness or squalor is permitted to exist anywhere, society must all be bad.

There must always be sin, and there must always be neglect and waste until we get to the millennium, which is not yet so near that we can see and feel it. In making our estimate of human progress, we must size up the whole situation and take the average condition. Similarly in attempting to remedy a local or special evil, we must avoid the injustice of unduly sacrificing the general welfare. By extreme measures planned to accomplish what may be good in the abstract but is still not practical, we can make the cause ridiculous.

Eugenic reformers, for instance, plan to rush right into regulation of human society and arrange marriages just as horses are bred at a stock farm. It has made some progress in Wisconsin, where they have required examination of those about to marry and certificates of health before issuing the marriage license. But I don't think the American people are quite ready to submit to that kind of regulation. If it could be enforced, it might be a good thing for the race, but a strong sentiment on the other side makes it impractical. In Wisconsin the law is being ignored and in foreign countries where restrictions upon marriages are rigorously enforced, marriage is dispensed with and concubinage results.

There is another feature of this present

hysterical condition that, I hope, is going to disappear. But we might as well recognize it. That is this wish to exculpate the sins of those who are unfortunate by putting the blame on society at large. The desire seems to be, if possible, to make scapegoats of those who are fortunate. It is this sentiment that has given rise to investigations into the coöperative stores in order to charge their managers with responsibility for the prostitution of some of their employees because of the wages they pay. As the investigation shows, there never was a more unfounded charge, but the very fact that it was used is an indication of what I mean. It manifests itself in the movement to dispense with all reticence and amplify in every way sex education on the theory that society is to blame because it is not telling young people of the danger of sin. You do not have to stand over a sewer and breathe in the bad smell in order to recognize that it has a bad smell when you meet it again.

I am strongly in favor of having young men and young women know certain things about sex matters, the young men through lectures in school or college, and the young women through instruction by women who can tell them in a short time all they need to know; but this idea of emphasizing and expanding the subject and of cultivating a free interchange of thoughts between the sexes is most dangerous. For one hundred years these subjects have been suppressed in America to the great benefit of society and it is well that they should remain so. So-called reforms in this direction are made the excuse for pruriency in drama, in novels, in moving pictures and in other ways that are distinctly vicious in their effect. They promote lubricity and although such literature and exhibitions may have the support of good people who think they are advocating great principles, they should be condemned.

Take another instance. Of course we all wish penitentiaries to be free from disease, and we are interested in prison reform to the extent of making them as healthful as possible for the prisoners. But this idea of making society a scapegoat and ridding everybody from responsibility for his sins, on the theory that his grandfather or grandmother was wicked and he is only doing it because of his heredity, makes the preservation of law and order impossible, and destroys the peace and comfort of those who are law-abiding. The penitentiary is a place for punishment and reformation. It is not a rest cure or a summer hotel. I have no doubt that prison discipline can be improved; but changes based on the theory that convicted criminals are disguised heroes who only need an appeal to their honor and freedom from restraint to make them good citizens will have humiliating but perhaps instructive results.

But these extravagances should not blind us to the real benefit of this growing sense of brotherhood among men. It is shown not only by the fact that it is preached in the pulpits and emphasized in the press and in magazines, but, still more, by the fact that it has been taken up by politicians. When they get hold of a subject and believe it needs elaboration, you may know that it has a lodgment with the people. Nor can we ignore the fact that this feeling has been increased by indignation at the political and social corruption incident to our enormous material development. The people have become ashamed of it in a sense.

With many, this growing sense of brotherhood stimulates the movement toward state socialism. Our excessive paternalism leads on to this. The view that the government can do anything, remedy every evil, level every inequality and make everybody happy, would have a most disastrous effect on production and individual effort and enterprise. The next step will be to curtail the right of property. It is difficult to define Socialism as a practical plan of government. The plan as set forth in a little book published in Austria called "The Quintessence of Socialism" is as definite as any that I know. It involves such governmental restriction of individual freedom of action and such real tyranny that the American people could not stand it. In fact, the regulation of the details of life by a system of awards for particular work, made by committees instead of by the operation of the law of supply and demand, would bring about a condition that would burst itself in a very little time. As "Billy" Sumner used to say, "If you have that kind of a system, I choose to be on the committee."

Another sign of the times is trades-unionism. Trades-unionism is essential in the cause of labor. One man as a laborer is in a position where it is utterly impossible for him to deal on an equality with his employer. The employer has capital and can get along without his services, but he cannot get along without the wages which the employer pays him. Therefore, laborers unite and contribute to a fund which enables them to withdraw together and say to the employer: "Here, we propose to deal with you on a level. We have great force. We have a fund which will enable us to live while out of work and we are going to embarrass you as far as possible by withdrawing from your employ unless you do justice to us in the matter of terms of service." That power of union cultivated in organized labor has done a great deal to raise wages and bring about equitable terms of service.

Organized labor is only a small part of labor generally; but organized labor exercises great influence in legislatures. It is thought to hold the balance of power at the polls and has undoubtedly exercised beneficent influence in securing laws to control healthy conditions for work, safety appliances on railroads, limitation upon the hours of labor and a number of other laws that would not have been passed if organized labor had not brought political influence to bear upon members of the legislature.

On the other hand, a sense of their power has sometimes given leaders of labor unions a lack of discretion, a truculence and an unreasonable and unjust attitude. Like the employers, they have been dependent upon public opinion and after a time public opinion has controlled them. Probably the greatest evil that stands out from all the good work unions have done, is the dead level to which they seek to bring the wages of skilled manual labor. Organized labor insists on making a class and then having that class receive the same wages, and it does nothing to encourage individual effort by consenting to the payment of higher wages to the man of experience, industry and skill than to the mediocre and lazy. It will in some way have to obviate that difficulty which works against the cause of labor and the interest of society. Moreover, its leaders do not discourage, as they should, lawlessness as a means of achieving their industrial ends. The history of the dynamiters in California and of the civil war in Colorado shows this.

On the other hand, we find many in the ranks of labor offering the most effective opposition to the increase in socialism. The leaders of trades-unionism have no sympathy with the I. W. W. The I. W. W., however, led by Haywood and others, serve a useful purpose by furnishing an awful example for the average workingman. When they go around with the signs, "No God, No Country, No Law," creating disgust and conservatism in the ranks of organized labor, they do not know what a good thing they are doing. They act blindly, but they are offering a sample of what may be expected if organized labor is tempted to excesses. We are going to have organized labor for all time, and we ought to have it. While I would go to the fullest extent with courts and even with the army to protect a non-union man in freedom of labor, if I were a workingman myself I would join a labor union because I believe that if such unions can be properly conducted, they are useful to promote the best interests of labor and of society. What trades-unionism needs is leaders to teach its members common sense.

The truth is, the longer you live, the more you will find that nothing is perfect, and everything has a side that can be criticised. What you have to do is to sum up the whole, take the average benefit which comes from it, and attempt to increase that average. Now I am an optimist. People say the initiative and the referendum, against which I have talked, are like a ratchet wheel. If you extend power to the people and the voters, you will never get it back again. I agree that is a rule that generally works, but with respect to the initiative and the referendum there is an element that may cause an exception to the rule. The initiative will throw a heavy burden on the electorate. Cranks and their followers will constantly be compelling voters to act upon wild proposals. As the popular disgust grows, the requirements in respect to the number of signers will be made so heavy that a successful petition can rarely be secured. The referendum will then be limited to such matters as the legislature chooses to refer and will then cease to be a practical burden.

We must pray that the injurious excesses which I have been describing as the cost we have to pay for a great reform, may not unsettle the foundation of our government and destroy the self-imposed restraint arranged in the Constitution to make that government just to the individual, to the minority and to those who do not vote. If we do not disturb those foundations, we can count on the common sense of the American people to bring them back to sane views, and we can rejoice and continue to rejoice in the preservation of a popular government that for one hundred and twenty-five years has vindicated its conservatism and justice before the world and will continue to do so forever.